SOUTHERN AFRICA

SOUTHERN AFRICA
SOUTH AFRICA, NAMIBIA, SWAZILAND, LESOTHO, AND BOTSWANA

BY RHODA BLUMBERG

FRANKLIN WATTS
New York | London | Toronto | Sydney | 1981
A FIRST BOOK

A GROLIER COMPANY

Cover design by Jackie Schuman

Photographs courtesy of:
Associated Press: p. 7; Wide World: p. 10;
United Nations: pp. 19, 24, 33; Sygma (Barrell): p. 30;
Sygma (Marlow): p. 54; WHO: p. 38; F.A.O. Photo: pp. 42, 48;
Photo Researchers (Michael Hayman): p. 44.

Maps courtesy of Vantage Art, Inc.

Library of Congress Cataloging in Publication Data

Blumberg, Rhoda.
Southern Africa.

Bibliography: p.
Includes index.
SUMMARY: Explores the history, economy,
social structure, and future prospects
of these five southern African countries.
1. Africa, Southern—Juvenile literature.
[1. Africa, Southern] I. Title.
DT729.5.B58   968   80–25020
ISBN 0–531–04278–2

For William Gottlieb
and
Daniel Lynn Blumberg

CONTENTS

SOUTHERN AFRICA

WESTERN
SAHARA

CAPE
VERDE

SENEGAL

GAMBIA

GUINEA
BISSAU

GUINEA

SIERRA LEONE

LIBERIA

MAURITANIA

MALI

UPPER
VOLTA

IVORY
COAST

GHANA

TOGO

BENIN

NIGER

NIGERIA

CAMEROON

CHAD

CENTRAL
AFRICAN REPUBLIC

SUDAN

DJIBOUTI

ETHIOPIA

SOMALIA

EQUATORIAL GUINEA

SAO TOME & PRINCIPE

GABON

CONGO

ZAIRE

UGANDA

KENYA

RWANDA
BURUNDI

TANZANIA

SEYCHELL

ANGOLA

ZAMBIA

MALAWI

MOZAMBIQUE

COMORO
ISLANDS

MADAGASCAR

MAURITI

REUNIO

NAMIBIA

ZIMBABWE

BOTSWANA

SWAZILAND

LESOTHO

SOUTH
AFRICA

Africa

1

SOUTH AFRICA: WHITE RULE ON A BLACK CONTINENT

Gold, diamonds, thriving industries! The Republic of South Africa is one of the richest countries in the world. But despite the glittering gems and growing wealth, it is a troubled nation.

Because the color of their skin is not white, over twenty-one million people are denied the most elementary rights. They cannot vote, and they cannot live or work where they choose. Hotels, restaurants, theaters, trains, buses, and schools are all segregated. White people make the laws and decisions. Four and a half million whites control a nation of twenty-six million.

It is shocking to read that the Republic of South Africa classifies everyone according to its own unique color chart. The government's official yearbook divides the population into four groups.

Blacks (71 percent of the population)
The term refers to African natives. The word *Bantu* is frequently used instead of *black, native,* or *African.* Bantus are natives who speak a Bantu language. Most tribes in southern Africa are Bantu-speaking people. Black natives do not like to be called Bantus, however. They prefer to be called Africans.

Asians (3 percent of the population)
Most Asians are descendants of Indian workers brought to South Africa in the middle of the nineteenth century to work on sugar plantations. Malaysians whose ancestors were imported as slaves, and Chinese whose forebears were recruited to work in gold and diamond mines, are also in this category.

Coloureds * (9 percent of the population)
Anyone who is part-white, part-black, or part-Asian and part-black is "coloured." Many coloureds are descendants of native Africans and early European settlers.

Whites (17 percent of the population)
Anyone not black, Asian, or coloured is white. In South Africa, the term *European* refers to white people.

White South African citizens are divided into two categories: English-speaking people, and Afrikaners.

English-speaking whites are those whose primary language is English. Most of them are of British descent. *Boer,* meaning "farmer" in Dutch, is the name applied to the early South Af-

*This is the British spelling, which is used in South Africa.

rican settlers of Dutch, German, and French descent. Today, descendants of the Boers are usually called *Afrikaners.* Their main language, *Afrikaans,* is derived from seventeenth-century Dutch, combined with African, English, German, and French words.

The country's official languages are Afrikaans and English. Both languages appear on public notices, and are taught in schools.

2
THE FIRST SETTLERS

Portuguese sailors were the first Europeans to see South Africa. They discovered it in 1488, when they rounded the Cape of Good Hope and found a new route to the Far East.

A Dutch ship's surgeon named Jan Van Riebeeck brought the first 125 white settlers to South Africa in 1652. He established a "refreshment station" at the Cape for the Dutch East India Company. The company's ships bound for the East Indies to collect precious spices, stopped at his station before sailing on to the Far East. The station supplied water, fresh vegetables grown by the settlers, and meat which was bartered from native Africans. The fresh food was urgently needed to prevent scurvy. At least one third of any crew sailing between Europe and the Indies used to suffer from scurvy, a disease caused by a diet lacking in vitamin C.

Van Riebeeck didn't intend to found a colony. He had strict

instructions to keep his station as small as possible—just a few houses, some vegetable gardens, a hospital, and a small fort. There was no need to expand, for although the land was breathtakingly beautiful and the climate most agreeable, the country seemed worthless. South Africa with its hidden treasures of diamonds and gold was, at the time, just a stopover for those seeking the Orient's riches of pepper, cinnamon, and cloves.

However, the station couldn't grow enough food to meet the needs of passing ships. Therefore, the Dutch East India Company invited Europeans to South Africa, offering free passage and free plots of land at the Cape Colony. They even imported orphan girls from the Netherlands to become wives of settlers. In addition to the Dutch and Germans, French Huguenots also emigrated to South Africa. The Huguenots belonged to a sect of Protestants who were fleeing from religious persecution in France.

Because native South Africans were usually unwilling to work for the settlers, the company decided to import slaves. The first twelve slaves arrived from the Dutch East Indies in 1657. The following year, 185 slaves were brought in from West Africa. As a result of an expanding slave trade, by the early eighteenth century, there were more slaves than white people at the Cape Colony. The slaves were used as domestics, carpenters, fishermen, and boat builders. Wheat and wine farmers were particularly dependent upon them to work their farms and harvest their crops.

By the end of the eighteenth century, there were about fifteen thousand Europeans in South Africa. Many of them claimed large tracts of land for themselves. Enormous areas not occupied by African tribes were free for the taking. And just as

*Hunting with a bow and arrow has long been
part of the traditional way of life for the
Bushmen of Southern Africa. Murdered by
European settlers and ravaged by poverty
and disease, only a few thousand remain today.*

American colonists took land from the Indians, the early white settlers grabbed territory that belonged to natives.

Bushmen and Hottentots were the first to suffer. The Bushmen, short tan-skinned people, fled from the white man's Cape Colony, to remote caves and deserts. Settlers hunted them down and shot them for sport. Disease also reduced their numbers. Since they were primitive hunters, only a few thousand Bushmen survive today. The Hottentots, also tan-skinned, but somewhat taller than the Bushmen, were expert herdsmen who had domesticated cattle, sheep, and goats. They fed and aided the first settlers, but were soon forced to hand over their animals and land. They became servants and shepherds for the colonists.

When the colonists set out for new territories along the East Coast, they encountered powerful resistance from the Bantus, who were a warlike people, well-armed and organized for battle. Many lives were lost during a series of terrible battles. The Bantus fought desperately to hold on to land they used for farms and cattle. But spear-throwing African warriors were no match for Boers using firearms. In 1780, the Boers and the Bantus signed a treaty making the Fish River in the southeast the boundary that separated them. Nevertheless, clashes between the Bantus and the Boers continued for almost one hundred years thereafter.

3
THE BOERS AND
THE BRITISH

In 1794, the Dutch East India Company went out of business because of poor management and the loss of trade to competing companies. A year later, British troops occupied the Cape. The Dutch regained control in 1803, but in 1806, the British returned to rule. At the Congress of Vienna in 1814, after the Napoleonic wars, the Cape Colony was formally given to England.

The Boers resented British rule. They opposed the new government's interest in helping the natives and people whose skin was not white. Boers believed that they were God's chosen people with a divine mission to dominate nonwhite "inferior races."

When English was made the official language of the Cape Colony in 1828, most of the Afrikaners took their children out of school rather than have them learn English. It wasn't only the

English language that was offensive to the Afrikaners. English law replaced Dutch law, and English money replaced Dutch currency.

The final blow came in 1833, when the British abolished slavery. Many Boer farmers were ruined when they had to give up their slave laborers.

Ridiculous rumors spread among the Boers that the British intended to encourage marriages between whites and blacks, that most of the land would be handed over to the Hottentots, and that all Dutch Reformed churches would be closed.

Thousands of families wanted to put as much distance as possible between themselves and the British government at the Cape. They packed their belongings and left in ox-drawn covered wagons, moving their cattle with them.

A mass migration known as the Great Trek began in 1835. Within nine years, at least fourteen thousand Boers had left the Cape Colony, determined to start a new life for themselves in the interior of southern Africa. Some traveled northeast into Natal, where native Zulus lived with their huge herds of cattle. Fierce Zulu warriors attacked them. In February 1838, after a series of bloody battles with the Zulus, Piet Retief, the Boer leader, thought he had arranged a peace treaty with the natives. A meeting to sign it was set up with the Zulu king, Dingane, who was supposed to hand over some land to the trekkers. Instead, Retief and sixty of his followers were murdered. Following this massacre, ten thousand Zulu warriors slaughtered Boer families living nearby.

Soldiers were sent up from the Cape Colony. In December 1838, they defeated the Zulus at the Battle of Blood River. The Zulus had to give up control of the entire district of Natal. King

Dingane was murdered by his own people. His brother, Mapande, the new king, was forced to accept the presence of the trekkers.

At last the Boers were able to establish a state of their own, the Republic of Natal. However, they enjoyed only a few years of independence. In 1842, the British attacked. A year later, the Boers surrendered, and in 1845, Natal became a province of the British Cape Colony.

Unhappy about British rule, many Natal farmers joined other trekkers in the north and west. These trekkers had also conquered lands belonging to Bantu tribes. This time, the British did not pursue them. They were not anxious to take over distant, seemingly worthless lands that required administrators and a strong military force to fight native tribes. As a result, the trekkers were allowed to establish two independent republics: the Transvaal, recognized in 1852, and the Orange Free State, recognized in 1854.

DIAMONDS AND GOLD

The British lack of interest in the Boer republics changed when diamonds were discovered in the Orange Free State, and when gold was found in the Transvaal.

A child named Erasmus Jacob is credited with discovering the first diamond. He picked up a pebble that proved to be a

Once the proud rulers of the province
that is now Natal, Zulus are now scattered
throughout poor villages in the area.

21-carat gem. His historic find, which took place in 1867, was worth a fortune. It was bought for £350 (less than $1,500). Two years later, a native found an 85-carat diamond. He sold his treasure for five hundred sheep, ten oxen, and one horse. This stone, known as "the Star of South Africa," is today one of the British Crown Jewels.

Thousands of fortune hunters came to dig in diamond fields that were to become the famous Kimberly Mines.

The British decided that, although the land seemed to be part of the Orange Free State, it was actually an area that was officially under their protection.

In order to stop all disputes about ownership, the British paid the Boers £90,000 ($360,000) for the diamond-rich land. Because the Orange Free State needed British-owned roads for transportation, it had no choice but to accept the money. However, the transaction made relations between the Boers and the British worse than ever.

Credit for the discovery of gold in the Transvaal goes to George Harrison, who hit pay dirt in 1886, when he was digging the foundation for a house. He found the Main Reef, the richest goldfield the world has ever known. Harrison was given £10 (less than $50) for his claim. His modest success started a gold rush. Adventurers poured into the Transvaal. They crowded in camps on the site that mushroomed into the city of Johannesburg.

Most of the gold diggers came from the Cape Colony and from England. The Boers called them "outlanders" (foreigners). By 1895, outlanders made up more than half of the Transvaal's white population.

To keep control of their government, the Boers gave very limited political rights to the outlanders. They were not allowed to vote for members of Parliament unless they resided in the Transvaal for fourteen years. Since prospectors usually left after staking mine claims, this meant that outlanders had no voice in the government.

Concern for the rights of the outlanders was the trumped-up reason for a plot to overthrow the Transvaal government. Cecil Rhodes, the diamond-rich prime minister of the Cape Colony, owned a private army. He convinced his friend Dr. Leander Jameson to lead this army into the city of Johannesburg in the Transvaal. Jameson was captured by the Boers and handed back to the Cape authorities as a criminal.

The nations of the world were shocked that Rhodes plotted an unprovoked attack against a small Boer state. Rhodes was forced to resign as prime minister. Jameson was arrested and sent to prison in London. The Jameson raid served only to intensify the hatred between the Boers and the British.

THE ANGLO-BOER WAR

Begun in 1899, the Anglo-Boer War was fought not only in the Transvaal and in the Orange Free State, but also in British-dominated Natal and in the Cape Colony. Boer farmers fought against the overwhelming might of the British Empire—seventy thousand Boer farmer-soldiers against three hundred thousand experienced British troops.

The British burned almost every Boer farm, destroying crops and livestock. But the worst scandal of the war was the condition of refugee camps. Twenty-six thousand women and children placed in these camps after their homes were destroyed by British troops died from lack of food and disease. After three years of fighting, a peace treaty was signed in 1902. The Boer republic of the Orange Free State lost its independence and became part of the British Empire.

THE REPUBLIC OF
SOUTH AFRICA

Afrikaners were determined to gain their independence. Their cause became popular among many sympathetic British South Africans.

In 1908, both Boer and British representatives drafted a constitution for a united country consisting of the Cape Colony, Transvaal, Natal, and the Orange Free State. The British Parliament approved, and in 1910, the Union of South Africa was created. It was a self-governing dominion within the British Empire, like the dominions of Canada, New Zealand, and Australia.

In 1961, South Africa left the Commonwealth and became the independent Republic of South Africa. A president replaced the queen of England as head of state.

The British were relieved to rid themselves of South Africa, for the country had become an embarrassment. Nonwhites from other nations of the Empire wanted nothing to do with the Afrikaner-dominated, racist country. In the Republic of South Africa, most political, economic, and social privileges continue to be for whites only.

4
SOUTH AFRICA TODAY

The Republic of South Africa is divided into four provinces: the Cape of Good Hope, Natal, Transvaal, and the Orange Free State. Each has its own Provincial Council. A 55-member Senate and a 165-member House of Assembly make up South Africa's Parliament. Its members are elected for a five-year term. The president, chosen by Parliament, serves seven years. He is advised by a cabinet headed by the prime minister. Only white candidates and white voters take part in elections. All key government positions are held by whites.

In 1980, the government announced that it would give non-whites representation in the government. The all-white Senate would be replaced by several consulting councils. There would be separate councils for blacks, coloureds, and Asians, each

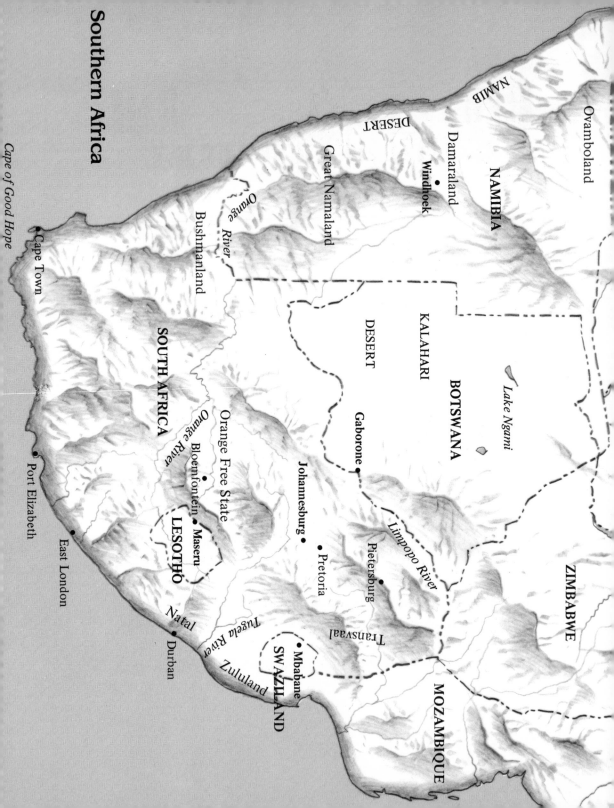

Southern Africa

Cape of Good Hope

Cape Town

Port Elizabeth

East London

Durban

Natal

Zululand

LESOTHO

Maseru

Bloemfontein

Orange Free State

Orange River

SOUTH AFRICA

Bushmanland

Orange River

Great Namaland

Damaraland

Windhoek

NAMIBIA

DESERT

NAMIB

Ovamboland

KALAHARI

DESERT

BOTSWANA

Lake Ngami

Gaborone

Johannesburg

Pretoria

Pietersburg

Limpopo River

Transvaal

Tugela River

Mbabane

SWAZILAND

MOZAMBIQUE

ZIMBABWE

allowed to offer suggestions and to express opinions. However, their powers were to be limited. They would only advise the white government, and not help to rule the country.

The National party has controlled the government since 1948. It receives its support from Afrikaners, and from English-speaking whites. The National party stands for white supremacy in politics and in business. It has always opposed attempts at social integration.

The main opposition party, the United party, also favors white rule, but it believes that all racial groups should be represented in Parliament.

Another important political party, the Progressive Reform party, is more liberal, believing that all people, regardless of skin color, should vote and have the opportunity to be elected.

Of the political parties formed by nonwhites, the African National Congress (ANC) is the most important. In 1960, the party was outlawed and its leaders were imprisoned without trial. The crackdown took place after members of the party participated in a demonstration against racist laws. During the demonstration, in the town of Sharpeville, police opened fire, killing sixty-nine people.

Although banned in South Africa, the African National Congress is still an active revolutionary force there. Whites, as well as nonwhites, play an important role. The party has offices in London, New York, and Tanzania. Many members work from Mozambique and other black countries, illegally entering South Africa, to arrange strikes, protest marches, and acts of violence.

The African National Congress admits that it has plotted

and participated in attacks against police stations, factories, and fuel supplies within South Africa. It has issued statements from foreign bases, taking responsibility for various bombings.

Not only the lack of political rights, but poverty and social oppression motivate people not associated with political parties to participate in strikes and protests. They contrast their poor dwellings with the beautiful homes of the many wealthy white people. They see luxurious beach resorts and magnificent golf clubs that they could never afford to enjoy. Even if they could afford these pleasures, such facilities are "for whites only."

In arguing their case for dominating the country, white citizens point out that America, Canada, Australia, and New Zealand were nations created by European settlers. They, too, founded their own nations. Why should anyone accuse white South Africans of being intruders? The country *is* theirs, not only because they colonized it, but because they have governed it for over three hundred years, and made it a rich country.

South Africa ranks among the half dozen richest nations of the world. White people take credit for developing the land, creating industries, and building modern cities, such as Johannesburg, Pretoria, and Cape Town.

The government points out that its natives enjoy a higher standard of living than blacks in other parts of Africa. And they call attention to their industries, which provide jobs for millions of black Africans. For example, more than four hundred thousand black men work in gold mines.

Cape Town, the chief port in South Africa.

As the most advanced country on the continent, it claims to be an economic boon to surrounding nations. South Africa exports food, machinery, and other necessities to its less-privileged neighbors. It has announced plans to build bridges, harness water, generate power, and irrigate land for other countries in Africa.

South African wealth is important to countries all over the world. What Saudi Arabia is to oil, South Africa may be to certain strategic raw materials. It is the United States' major supplier of chrome, a metal needed to produce a variety of steels. Platinum is another important metal used in refining gasoline, and in making electrical switches. The supply of these metals is critical to the United States and other Western nations, because the other major source of chrome and platinum is the Soviet Union.

South Africa is the world's largest supplier of gold, and an important source of diamonds, uranium, copper, coal, and asbestos. Since 1910, the production of minerals has been doubling every ten years.

The country has the only commercial plants that extract liquid fuels from coal. This is a technology which many other nations, including the United States, may need, if they are to reduce their dependence on imported fuels.

Despite its importance as a world power, the future of South Africa is clouded by the many problems caused by the government's treatment of its nonwhite population.

5
LIVING APART

The practice of white supremacy in South Africa has been official since 1974, when the doctrine of apartheid was adopted as government policy.

Apartheid, pronounced a-*part*-hate, means "apart-ness," or "separate development." It is supposed to mean that all blacks will eventually own territories and will have the right to rule themselves. But first, they must prove they are capable of self-rule, and even then, the white government has final supreme control.

HOMELANDS
The Republic has carved the map of their country into separate areas for whites and blacks. Territories set aside for blacks are called homelands, or Bantustans. They are supposed to promote tribal life, and allow blacks the chance to develop their own independent nations.

In reality, the homelands are nothing more than native reservations on the poorest, least-desirable land in South Africa. So much of the territory of these homelands is mountainous or desertlike that people are unable to grow enough food for their families. Hunger is commonplace. Those areas with good soil are so overcrowded that not enough food can be cultivated for the population.

Homelands take up 13 percent of the land. Most homelands lack not only good soil, but mineral resources and industries. Eighty-seven percent of the country's richest, most fertile territory is reserved for white citizens, who enjoy plentiful crops and thriving businesses.

Homelands are jam-packed with pathetically poor people. They are occupied mainly by women, children, and men too old or too sick to work. Most able-bodied males over the age of fifteen don't live with their families. They must take jobs in mines and factories far from their homelands, and they are usually away from their families from nine months to one year at a time. Mine workers are housed in all-male barracks, often twenty to a room. Some factories have similar barracks. About two million black males are continuously absent from their homes in the homelands.

The government of South Africa assigns all Africans to homelands. It has set up ten homelands, supposedly representing ten different tribes, each with its own distinct culture and language. Actually, the natives of South Africa belong to hundreds of tribes and speak an enormous variety of dialects.

Millions of blacks from various parts of South Africa have been notified that they must move to an assigned homeland.

For example, 1.6 million blacks scattered all over the country were told that they were no longer citizens of the Republic of South Africa. Because they were Xhosa- and Sotho-speaking people, their homeland was to be Transkei. Transkei is an area most of them had never seen.

People were forced to move their households great distances from homes their families and ancestors had occupied. Many who had lived peacefully for four generations on land purchased over a hundred years ago, were ordered to move to a place chosen for them by South African officials.

Blacks have received as little as a day's notice before being piled on trucks and moved hundreds of miles away. In many cases, their homes are then deliberately destroyed by bulldozers or by fire.

In the 1960s, blacks were ordered to leave their homes on the south side of the Tugela River and move to the less desirable north side. When they resisted, police burned their huts. They were forced to become citizens of Kwa-Zulu, a poor, overcrowded homeland across the river.

During the past twenty-five years, two million blacks have been uprooted and resettled. Before the government's plans are completed, another million blacks will be removed to homelands by South African officials.

The practice of moving people is known as black-spot removal. Black spots are black settlements in urban white areas. Blacks are forced out of white districts, and from land wanted by whites. People throughout the world are outraged at these practices. After an international protest in 1979, the South African government abandoned plans to bulldoze Cross Roads, a

black settlement of twenty-four thousand, near Cape Town. Because of a worldwide public outcry in this case, the residents did not have to move.

When Africans are assigned to a homeland, they become citizens of that homeland. They are no longer citizens of the Republic of South Africa, and they cannot vote in government elections. Black people are therefore denied citizenship in their native land. They are foreigners in their own country.

In theory, the South African government is offering them territory where they can own land and govern themselves. In reality, the South African government still controls them. Although residents of homelands have their own chiefs and native councils, they are supervised by the white Department of Bantu Affairs. Homeland chiefs have limited power. They can try petty civil and criminal cases, and settle minor disputes about land. The chiefs receive their salaries from the South African government—a factor that keeps many of them from assuming too much power.

The white Department of Bantu Affairs makes all the major decisions. It can issue orders requiring entire tribes to move from one place to another. Residents feel imprisoned, for they are not allowed to leave their homelands without a special permit, and outsiders can't visit without permission from South African officials.

Ninety-seven separate blocks of territory scattered around South Africa make up the ten homelands. For example, the Ciskei

A typical house in the black settlement of Cross Roads.

homeland has seventeen districts, and the Kwa-Zulu homeland has forty-two areas, separated from each other by white-occupied land.

The South African government has stated that eventually each homeland will be more unified. Its goal for the near future is to allocate thirty-four parcels of property for the ten homelands.

Critics insist that the white government has deliberately divided the blacks geographically, to prevent them from becoming unified. The South African government has the power to fix boundaries and carve up the map as it chooses.

INDEPENDENT HOMELANDS

Eventually, all homelands are expected to become independent nations. But first, they must prove to the Republic of South Africa that they are ready and able to rule themselves.

Three homelands have received so-called independence. They are Transkei, Venda, and Bophuthatswana. These countries have their own flags, national anthems, and official languages. South Africa claims that they are foreign countries, yet it retains the right to control their foreign affairs and defense. It also helps them with "foreign aid"—funds which it can cut off when it chooses. It did just that during a border dispute not long ago with Transkei.

Most nations of the world, and most Africans, consider "homeland independence" trickery on the part of South Africa. White South Africa rids itself of black citizens through its policy of creating new nations. The homeland, Kwa-Zulu, refuses the so-called independent status. It declares that South Africa just wants to dump 5.5 million Zulu citizens by making them members of a Kwa-Zulu nation.

The United Nations Special Committee Against Apartheid has denounced the new states of Transkei, Venda, and Bophuthatswana. Most governments, including the United States, refuse to recognize them.

Indians and coloureds don't have homelands. However, they too must live in areas separated from whites and suffer from discrimination in education, employment, and civil rights.

TOWNSHIPS

Officially, blacks aren't allowed permanent homes in white areas. Although a few do live among whites, most city dwellers live in townships. Townships are black ghetto extensions of cities and towns. Black families are permitted to remain in townships if they were born there, or if they have permanent jobs nearby.

At least 3.5 million blacks live in townships. They are employed in private white homes, factories, mines, and businesses. Most of them commute by bus to their jobs.

Soweto, just outside the city of Johannesburg, is the largest of these townships. About 1.2 million blacks live there in shacks. A typical shack has no bathroom, no hot water, and no electricity.

In 1976, racial tensions exploded in Soweto. An orderly march of young blacks demanding better schools turned into a riot. Police used gunfire to stop them. After three days of disorder, over one hundred blacks were killed, and more than one thousand were injured. The turmoil spread to townships in other parts of the country, where conditions are just as overcrowded and miserable. At least seven hundred blacks lost their lives.

A growing wave of protests and violence over the last several years has raised fears that the country may be headed for large-scale revolt.

[27]

6
JUSTICE, SKIN-DEEP

The white South African government always treated nonwhites as inferiors. People can measure their privileges by their skin color. Indians are slightly better off than coloureds, who are somewhat better off than blacks. All receive shabby treatment.

White people have social, political, and economic advantages that are denied to others. To insure their privileged position, more than three hundred antiblack laws are on the books. Most of these laws apply to Asians and "coloured" people, too.

Hotels, theaters, beaches, restaurants, railroads, and buses keep the races segregated. There is a Prohibitions of Mixed Marriages Act. When it was passed in 1949, men and women of different races who had been married for years and who refused to separate from each other were arrested and imprisoned for breaking the law. An Immorality Amendment Act forbids sexual relations between whites and nonwhites.

The Natives Act of 1952 requires everyone over sixteen to carry a passbook which contains a photograph, and details about race, residence, and job. Being found without one's passbook is a criminal offense. Anyone discovered in a white area without a permit in his or her passbook is also breaking the law. Thousands of men and women are arrested and imprisoned every year for passbook offenses.

WORK RESTRICTIONS

Blacks must secure official permission to accept or change jobs. They receive poor wages. As a rule, a black receives an income that is only 10 to 15 percent that of a white. They have little hope of bettering themselves because there are laws that forbid their employment as skilled laborers in mines and in many factories. At any rate, they usually don't qualify for better jobs because they have never been properly trained or educated. South Africa has two million blacks who are unemployed; coloureds, Asians and whites account for about another thirty thousand unemployed.

Recently, blacks have been allowed to become members of trade unions. However, they have little power, for any protest against their conditions could lead to arrest. In 1980, when there was a strike at the Ford Motor Company in Port Elizabeth, black leaders were arrested and imprisoned.

According to law, children under the age of sixteen are not allowed to work. In the case of black children however, the law is not strictly enforced. Black children work as domestic servants, as farmhands, and as workers in shops. They receive meager wages.

*Through the efforts of a largely black
work force, South Africa has become the
largest diamond producer in the world.*

SEPARATE EDUCATION

Education for white children is required by law and is free. Before 1981, black children didn't have to go to school, and their parents had to pay part of the cost of educating them.

Over 51 percent of the African children receive no education at all. Their parents can't afford to pay for it. Those who do attend receive an education that doesn't compare in quality with the schooling received by white children. The South African government spends fifteen times more to educate a white child than a black child.

The color bar is also a barrier that keeps blacks out of various training and vocational schools. Why educate people for skilled jobs they are not allowed to have?

SEPARATE HEALTH CARE

Apartheid is a disease that even affects the practice of medicine. Studies published by the United Nations show that there is one doctor for every forty-four thousand African children, compared with one doctor for every four hundred white children. Blacks use separate ambulances, and separate and inferior hospital facilities.

POLITICAL PRISONERS

Blacks run the risk of arrest for an offense as minor as membership in a political organization. Some blacks have been imprisoned for simply distributing leaflets. Anyone who publicly opposes apartheid risks arrest. Many white South Africans who sympathize with the oppression of nonwhites are banned.

Banning is a punishment that restricts a person indoors on nights and on weekends. Banned people are not permitted to meet with more than one person at a time (not including their family). They cannot publish writings or be quoted by newspapers. Banning is the mildest form of punishment. Activists who oppose government policy are usually arrested and imprisoned for breaking a law.

The Internal Security Act forbids any activity directed against "the security of the State"; the Unlawful Organization Act can prevent political rallies; the Sabotage Act is aimed against any attempt to damage the State; and the Terrorism Act guards against efforts for social and political change. These four repressive laws, in effect, guarantee that a legal excuse can be found for arresting anyone.

Under the Terrorism Act, a person of any race can be detained for up to ninety days without trial, without bail, and without access to a lawyer. After ninety days, the prisoner can be released and rearrested immediately for another ninety days. This may go on indefinitely. "Detainees" are often placed in solitary confinement. In some cases, torture accompanies questioning.

In 1977, a noted black leader named Steve Biko died of head wounds during police questioning. He had been detained in prison for opposing apartheid laws. There was a worldwide outcry when the news of his death became known. Biko had organized a fund to aid political prisoners. He was the founder of the Black Consciousness Movement and the South African

In downtown Johannesburg passengers board a bus for "non-Europeans only."

[32]

Students' Organization, whose aims were to stop racial discrimination. Seeking peaceful rather than violent means of change, Biko was loved in Africa the way Martin Luther King, Jr., was loved in the United States. Thousands of blacks and diplomats from thirteen Western nations attended his funeral.

No figures are available to show how many men, women, and children are now serving sentences for political offenses. Families of those arrested are not always notified. At the present time, there are at least five hundred political prisoners. Many are serving life sentences. Liberal whites, as well as nonwhites, have fled from the Republic of South Africa because of these oppressive laws.

WHEN WILL APARTHEID END?

For years, the United Nations has protested against the apartheid laws. In 1977, the Security Council imposed an arms embargo against South Africa. Most countries not only ban exports of military equipment, but, officially, they refuse to give South Africa economic assistance.

However, private companies are not prevented from doing business. Industries in the United States, Great Britain, West Germany, and Japan are major investors. The main fields of investments are mining, oil refineries, chemicals, metals, the automobile industry, textiles, paper, and pulp.

The South African government realizes that changes in its policy of racial separation must be made to insure its continued economic growth, and to prevent riots like the 1976 Soweto uprising.

Labor laws are being changed to permit nonwhites to join and form trade unions, to provide them with better pay, and to enable them to be trained and hired for skilled jobs. Segregation rules are being eased. Some restaurants, theaters, and hospitals are being opened to nonwhites. Factories are integrating cafeterias and social halls. Black leaders are being consulted about needed reforms.

But there have been no major changes. The hated apartheid laws remain on the books, and for the most part, they are still enforced.

7
NEIGHBORING COUNTRIES: THREE INDEPENDENT, DEPENDENT NATIONS

Three territories that were once ruled by the British are now black-ruled, independent nations. They are Botswana, Lesotho, and Swaziland. Although these countries sharply oppose apartheid, they must maintain friendly relations with their neighbor, the Republic of South Africa. They are still dependent upon this powerful country for jobs, food, imports, and financial help.

Despite their desire to be completely separated from a racist regime, important lifelines link them to it. Botswana, Lesotho, and Swaziland are joined with South Africa in a Customs Union Agreement. South Africa levies and collects taxes on their imports. Each country then receives a share of the money. Because the customs union places a high tariff on imports from other countries, products from South Africa are cheaper. Therefore, Botswana, Lesotho, and Swaziland buy most of their goods from South Africa.

Their geographic closeness, economic needs, and political weakness require that the small countries maintain a working relationship with the rich, powerful Republic of South Africa. Botswana, Lesotho, and Swaziland are indeed independent, dependent nations.

THE REPUBLIC OF BOTSWANA

Slightly smaller than the state of Texas, with only about eight hundred thousand people, Botswana is a landlocked country completely surrounded by South Africa, Namibia, Zambia, and Zimbabwe.

Most of the land is covered by the Kalahari Desert, which has grassy plains and low bushes, as well as sand dunes. Several thousand Bushmen manage to survive there, living in caves and in temporary shelters. They eat plant roots and game, which they hunt with poison-tipped arrows. Many scientists believe that the Bushmen are the oldest living race.

The vast majority of the population are Batswanas. They live along the eastern "green strip" of the country, raising cattle. Only a small part of their land can be used for agriculture. Crop production is limited by the small amount of rainfall and the lack of irrigation. The most fertile areas are not owned by blacks but belong to British and Dutch families who acquired their property from the Africans during the late nineteenth century.

Botswana suffers from severe droughts that ruin crops and pastures. In the past, people and cattle have died of starvation when the rains failed to come. *Pula* is the Bantu word for rain. It is so meaningful that people say "pula" when greeting each other. Pula is also the name of the country's currency.

*Health care workers travel from home to home
to offer essential medical care to families in Botswana.*

History

Botswana was formerly called Bechuanaland. Little is known about the country's history before European travelers and missionaries arrived during the nineteenth century. David Livingstone, the famous explorer, was one of the missionaries who worked in Botswana.

During the nineteenth century, the Batswana people suffered from tribal wars. In 1872, when Khama III became their chief, he united them, built a strong army, and ended the warfare.

Chief Khama also succeeded in protecting his people against Boer trekkers who were settling on their land. The Boers were especially interested in the country when gold was found in the Tati region. The missionaries were anxious to help the natives keep their country for themselves. They encouraged Chief Khama to ask the British government for help in keeping the Boers from taking over their territory.

In 1885, Chief Khama willingly allowed his country to become the British Protectorate of Bechuanaland. As a native ruler, he still had power. However, a British high commissioner was appointed to govern the country. Bechuanaland's name was changed to Botswana in 1966, the year it became an independent nation.

Independence

The Republic of Botswana is a democracy headed by a president who is chosen in a national election for a five-year term. Its constitution provides for a thirty-six member National Assembly—thirty-two members directly elected by the people, four elected by the members themselves. There is a House of Chiefs made up of chiefs of the eight principal tribes, plus four others selected by subchiefs. The National Assembly cannot pass any bill relating to tribal matters without the approval of the House of Chiefs.

The Botswana government must balance its dependence upon South Africa against its hatred of that country's racial policies. Thus, it has no formal diplomatic relations with South Africa, and it refuses to recognize Transkei, Bophuthatswana and Venda, which were formerly homelands.

Botswana has been a haven for political activists who have fled from South Africa fearing arrest. However, although they are permitted to stay, the refugees are not allowed to be politically active. Botswana cannot afford to anger a country it needs for its own survival.

Botswana is heavily financed by its rich neighbor. Diamond mines that were discovered in Botswana are operated by South African companies. These companies are owned by major foreign investors who are also developing vast deposits of copper and nickel inside Botswana.

South Africa is the number-one customer for cattle and beef, its main export. The country's entire oil supply comes from South African refineries. Eighty-five percent of its total needs are imported from South Africa, and more than half of its exports are sold there.

Thousands of men leave Botswana for jobs in South Africa, where they are employed as unskilled workers in gold, coal, and diamond mines.

American interest in this tiny, struggling democracy is demonstrated by aid that runs to about $16 million a year, and by many Peace Corps volunteers who are teaching the Batswanas new skills.

[40]

THE KINGDOM OF LESOTHO

Lesotho, a tiny country about the size of Maryland, is completely surrounded by the Republic of South Africa. Because its 1.2 million people depend upon South Africa for survival, it has often been referred to as a "hostage state."

The country is very poor. Most of Lesotho is mountainous, and only about one tenth of its land can be used to grow crops. The people must import large quantities of food from South Africa in order to have enough to eat.

A 1 mile (1.61 km) railway links Lesotho with South African railroads. Because the country is landlocked, all goods must be shipped through South Africa. Lesotho has been called an island in a sea of apartheid.

There aren't enough jobs in Lesotho. About half its men must live in South Africa, employed there as miners, farmers, and industrial workers. They are migrants with contracts that keep them away from home for six to twelve months at a time.

Although an independent, black-ruled nation, Lesotho is in many ways like a homeland. At least two hundred thousand able-bodied males are absent. Women and children remain at home. They cultivate the fields and take care of the livestock. The lack of manpower, poor soil, and frequent droughts make life difficult.

History

Lesotho had a small population of primitive Bushmen until the end of the sixteenth century. Then tribal wars in Southern Africa caused refugees to seek protection in the mountains of Lesotho.

Chief Moshoeshoe (pronounced moSHWAy shay) is the country's national hero. He led many of the refugees from the

interior of South Africa into Lesotho and united these up-rooted people. His followers became known as the Basotho. Chief Moshoeshoe used peaceful means to stop attacks from Zulu warriors. He made peace with Shaka, the powerful Zulu chief, by sending him gifts of cattle.

After the threat of Zulu attacks ended, Moshoeshoe was faced with another enemy—the Boers. When the Boers trekked northward away from the Cape Colony, they threatened to take possession of the Basotho's land. Moshoeshoe decided to make the British an ally. He signed a treaty with them, hoping to be protected against the Boers.

Much to his dismay, Chief Moshoeshoe soon realized that the only way the British would guarantee his country's safety was by making it the British territory of Basutoland. First governed by the Cape Colony, in 1884, it became a member nation of the British Commonwealth.

In 1966, Basutoland attained full independence as the Kingdom of Lesotho.

Independence

There were political conflicts as soon as Lesotho became independent. The king and the prime minister engaged in a struggle for power. King Moshoeshoe II, great-grandson of the nation's

*Children on their way to school
in the mountainous region
of the Sani Pass, which links
Lesotho with South Africa.*

hero, objected to Prime Minister Leabua Jonathan's ideas. The prime minister believed that a "bread-and-butter good-neighbor policy" towards South Africa was in the best interests of his people. He advised his people to "think with their stomachs" and keep in mind that South Africa supplies food and jobs. King Moshoeshoe opposed friendship with a country that practiced apartheid.

In 1970, after losing the country's first national election, Prime Minister Jonathan seized control of the government. He declared a state of emergency, canceled the authority of the courts, and placed the king under house arrest. King Moshoeshoe was eventually permitted to go into exile in the Netherlands.

When Britain refused to recognize Jonathan's new government, and threatened to cut off the financial aid it had been giving to Lesotho, the king was permitted to return. However, his powers were limited, and he was not allowed to be politically active. Moshoeshoe became a puppet king, impressive only during ceremonies.

Although the government is called a constitutional monarchy, the constitution has not been in use since 1970. The prime minister rules. Since his takeover, Prime Minister Jonathan stopped several outbreaks of rebellion. Riots, bombings, and plots against him have taken place from time to time.

Listed as one of the twenty-five least-developed (poorest)

*A young cattle herder in Lesotho
uses a termite hill as an oven
to cook corn on the cob.*

nations of the world, Lesotho receives financial aid from the United Nations. The United States also contributes over $10 million each year to help this small, struggling country.

THE KINGDOM OF SWAZILAND

This beautiful little country is surrounded on the north, west, south, and southeast by the Republic of South Africa, and on the northeast by Mozambique. Smaller than Botswana and Lesotho, Swaziland is about the size of Connecticut, with a population of about half a million.

It is better off than most new countries in Africa. Swaziland has rich mineral deposits, valuable forests, some factories, large farms that raise cotton, tobacco, and sugar, and a booming tourist trade.

However, most of the mines, factories, farms, and hotels are owned by white Europeans or by South Africans. Today, 43 percent of the land is owned by white people, many of whom don't even live in Swaziland.

Seventy-five percent of the Swazi people eke out a living farming small plots of land, and raising cattle. They are peasant-farmers who measure their wealth by the number of cattle they own.

Like Botswana and Lesotho, Swaziland is economically dependent upon South Africa. More than 90 percent of its imports come from its rich neighbor. It needs South Africa as a customer for its own products. Sugar, wood pulp, iron, asbestos, and beef, are its main exports.

Swaziland, with its magnificent mountain scenery, is also a playground for rich South Africans who go there for its resort hotels and gambling casinos.

Over twenty-nine thousand citizens of Swaziland live in

South Africa, working in mines, industries, and farms. Absentee fathers are a problem for families in Swaziland, as they are in South African homelands and in Botswana and Lesotho.

History
The Swazi settled in their country during the early 1800s, after fleeing land that was being attacked by Zulus. When Zulus conducted raids inside Swaziland, the natives appealed to the British for protection. In return for this protection, British farmers were allowed to settle and own property in their country.

In the 1880s, after gold was discovered in Swaziland, hundreds of white prospectors convinced the Swazis to sign away rights to their land. The natives could not read, and they didn't realize that by marking a piece of paper they were giving away valuable property.

Both Great Britain and South Africa kept assuring the Swazi that their country would always be free and independent. However, in 1894, South Africa took over, and after the Anglo-Boer War in 1903, government rule was turned over to the British.

Under them, the Swazi enjoyed a fair amount of self-rule. Because they feared that South Africa would once again take control of their government, the British agreed to prepare Swaziland for independence. Although white residents tried to arrange separate elections for whites and blacks, the British government refused to let skin color affect politics.

Independence
Swaziland became an independent, constitutional monarchy in 1968. Unfortunately, in 1974, King Sobhuza did away with the constitution. He suspended meetings of the Parliament, out-

A young Swazi couple and their baby at home.

lawed political parties and political meetings, and made himself an all-powerful monarch.

Since that time, the king has reigned as supreme ruler. Interestingly enough, many Swazi uphold his right to be dictator, for according to tradition, the king has divine authority to be chief of state. He has a special spiritual role, and is considered both the political and religious leader.

The social system resembles the feudal society that existed in Europe during the Middle Ages. The king rules the land, aided by chiefs who control various districts. Each chief is a noble lord who has the right to demand free labor and gifts of food from people in his area. At harvesttime it is customary to give the chief one bag of whatever has been reaped from each field. This is usually maize or sorghum, a cereal grass.

There were hopes that the government would become more liberal in 1978. In that year, the king arranged for elections and a new constitution. However, much to the dismay of people who wanted reforms, the absolute authority of the king remained unchanged. The names of all candidates were sent to the king for his approval. There was no secret ballot. Under the new constitution, political parties were forbidden, and the role of Parliament was limited to advising the king.

An underground movement named Swanlu opposes the monarchy. Since 1978, antigovernment riots have been taking place. When the present king dies (he is presently in his eighties), there is little doubt that the structure of the government will change.

8
NAMIBIA

Namibia is the name of a country formerly known as South-West Africa. The land was named Namibia by the United Nations in 1968, when it was declared to be international territory, separate and free from the Republic of South Africa. However, South Africa continues to rule the country, which it still calls South-West Africa.

South Africa refuses to recognize the United Nation's authority. It has been controlling Namibia's government for over sixty years. And although it claims to be preparing that country for independence, South Africa shows few signs of releasing its tight grip on the territory.

Namibia is a land well-worth keeping. Its huge mineral resources include diamonds, uranium, lead, copper, and zinc. White settlers have developed large commercial farms and a profitable fishing industry. About one hundred thousand white settlers control much of the country's wealth. Unskilled labor is drawn from the native population of more than nine hundred thousand blacks.

Namibia is bordered on the north by Angola and Zambia, and by Botswana on the east—all black-ruled, independent nations. The Atlantic Ocean washes its western shores, and the Republic of South Africa adjoins it on the southeast and south.

Most of the land is desert. The Kalahari Desert in the east is occupied by a small number of Bushmen. The Namib Desert, stretching along the entire coast, is largely uninhabited. You can travel through it for hundreds of miles and never see another human being. Namibia's natives eke out a living farming and herding cattle in the central region.

HISTORY

The first Europeans to land on Namibia's shores were fifteenth-century Portuguese sea merchants. Because desert travel was risky, Europeans didn't explore the country until the late eighteenth century. At the beginning of the nineteenth century, German missionaries, emboldened by religious zeal, entered the territory. German traders, settlers, and officials followed.

In 1883, a German merchant built a trading station in South-West Africa. The following year, the country was officially made the German Protectorate of South-West Africa. Only the Walvis Bay area, which had been claimed by the British in 1878, was excluded. (Walvis Bay, part of South Africa today, has the territory's only deep-water port.)

By the beginning of the twentieth century, German settlers had grabbed the best land and taken most of the cattle from the Herero and Ovambo tribes.

Provoked after learning that the government intended to build a railroad through their land, and move them to a reservation, the Herero people declared war against the Germans in 1904. German soldiers practically wiped out the Hereros. It is estimated that sixty thousand lost their lives. Some of the survivors fled to Botswana.

In 1915, during World War I, South African armed forces, which were fighting on the side of the Allies, seized South-West Africa. As a reward, they expected that the country would be handed over to them when the war ended. But the League of Nations didn't allow this to happen. Instead, South-West Africa was declared international territory, assigned to South Africa as a "Class C Mandate." This meant that the country was to be administered by South Africa, which was expected "to promote to the utmost the material and moral well-being and social progress of the inhabitants of the territory."

South Africa never lived up to this mandate. It applied racial laws to its neighbors.

When the League of Nations came to an end in 1946, South Africa asked the newly formed United Nations for permission to make Namibia part of South Africa. The United Nations General Assembly rejected the request, and decided to make Namibia a trust territory, a country placed under the authority and administration of the United Nations. South Africa refused to respect this decision.

In 1966, the United Nations General Assembly once again declared that Namibia was to be administered by the United Nations. The following year, it appointed a council to be in charge until the country was ready for independence. South Africa never allowed the council to enter Namibia.

Under increasing international pressure, South Africa, in

1975, arranged the Turnhalle Conference, to draft a constitution for an independent Namibia. The conference was composed of white, coloured, and black leaders known to favor South African domination. The group recommended that Namibia be made up of states divided along tribal and racial lines. Such a plan was, of course, unacceptable to the Namibians.

In 1977, the United States, Britain, France, Canada, and West Germany detailed plans for elections in Namibia. But South Africa announced that it had its own plans for elections, which it proceeded to hold in 1978. The election was won by a party called the Democratic Turnhalle Alliance. The elections, boycotted by many groups in Namibia, were declared illegal by the United Nations.

Despite the many efforts of the United Nations and the Western powers to find a solution, South Africa stubbornly refuses to release its hold on its neighbor.

In 1979, the United Nations voted to have its member nations stop trading with South Africa until it permitted free, United Nations-supervised elections in Namibia. Because of South Africa's illegal occupation, the United States has no official diplomatic representative in Namibia, and it has no Peace Corps there.

WHITE RULE

Namibia's executive power is in the hands of an administrator, appointed by the President of South Africa. A Legislative Assembly is elected by Namibian citizens. Only whites may vote. Final authority for all matters rests with the South African government. The armed forces, police, and foreign affairs are directly controlled by South Africa.

Apartheid has thus been brought across the border. Nami-

bians suffer from many of the same disgraceful conditions that exist in South Africa.

There are two court systems: one for whites and westernized nonwhites, and one for natives. There are three separate school systems: one for whites, one for coloureds, and one for blacks. Ten times more money is spent to educate a white child than a coloured child. Twenty times more is spent for a white child than for a black child.

White children must attend school while black children don't have to receive an education. Consequently, a large number of them never learn to read and write.

There is no college in Namibia. White students usually go to a university in South Africa. The few blacks and coloureds who manage to graduate from high school can attend the United Nations Institute for Namibia, located in Zambia.

In recent years, some reforms in the apartheid laws have taken place. For example, the Mixed Marriages Act and the Immorality Act no longer apply to Namibia. Theaters, restaurants, and other public places have been open to all—in theory. But there are still public swimming pools, libraries, hotels, and restaurants that are closed to nonwhites, and the government does not impose penalties for this discrimination.

Blacks live in separate areas. All-black townships have miserable shacks with no running water and no electricity.

Namibia held its first free elections in December, 1978. The elections were finally declared illegal by the United Nations, however.

HOMELANDS

Homelands have been established for natives of Namibia. Like those in South Africa, they are poor and overcrowded.

Ovamboland, containing almost half the total black population, became the first homeland given "self-governing" status. South African advisors are really in control. Ovamboland supplies most of the black workers for Namibian diamond mines. After they sign work contracts, airplanes take them to mines far from home. They usually stay away eight months at a time.

Because there are no job opportunities in homelands, many blacks sign contracts to work on fishing vessels, or on distant commercial farms. A good many work as miners across the border, in South Africa.

No matter where they live and work, they are citizens of their assigned homelands. They can be arrested if they leave their jobs without permission.

The same type of passbook system used in South Africa is used in Namibia. Failure to carry complete identification can lead to arrest and imprisonment. No Africans dare leave their homelands or job areas without permits attached to their passbooks.

POLITICAL REPRESSION

South Africa's Terrorism Act controls political activities in Namibia. People opposing the government have been arrested, flogged in public, and imprisoned. An unknown number of political prisoners are now serving life sentences.

There have been up to forty different political parties opposing South African rule. The Namibian National Front is a group made up of whites, as well as nonwhites, who oppose segregation, and favor immediate independence. The South-West African People's Organization (SWAPO) is the most powerful political opponent of white rule. The United Nations recognizes SWAPO as the principal group voicing the wishes of native Namibians; SWAPO's primary opponent is the Democratic Turnhalle Alliance (DTA), which favors South African rule.

Because they fear arrest in their own country, members of SWAPO make their headquarters in neighboring Angola. SWAPO has gained support from people all over the world. It is backed by communist money and military equipment.

THE FIGHT FOR FREEDOM

Ever since 1966, black freedom fighters have been battling South African soldiers inside Namibia. The Republic of South Africa has at least twenty-five military bases there, and an army of between twenty thousand and fifty thousand soldiers. Approximately thirty-five hundred guerilla fighters are waging war against them. The People's Liberation Army of Namibia (PLAN) is organized by SWAPO.

Ambushes, land-mine explosions, and raids against white property owners have become common occurrences. Fighting has spilled over to Angola, and South African military attacks have been made against SWAPO bases there. Angola claims to have suffered many civilian deaths and damages amounting to over $300 million.

The United Nations Security Council has condemned South Africa's military actions in Angola. South Africa defends its aggression by pointing out that they must conquer communist fighters who want to control the entire African continent.

Bloodshed continues. SWAPO freedom fighters continue their battle against South African soldiers and police.

The future of Namibia remains uncertain. A peaceful solution could reduce the chances of a communist takeover. On the other hand, failure to settle racial unrest guarantees further bloodshed both in Namibia and in South Africa.

FOR FURTHER READING

Addison, John. *Ancient Africa*. New York: The John Day Company, 1970.

Balow, Tom, and Carpenter, Allan. *Botswana*. Chicago: Children's Press, 1973.

———. *Lesotho*. Chicago: Children's Press, 1975.

Carpenter, Allan, and Maginnis, Matthew. *Swaziland*. Chicago: Children's Press, 1970.

The Encyclopedia of Africa. New York: Franklin Watts, 1976.

INDEX